How to Make Healthy Sodas

Other books by Dale H. Gillilan
Bright Lines Journal: Fast Ways to
Powerful Changes
Bright Line Eating Sodas

This is a **Healthy Living™** book from
ToolsForTheJourney.com
#HealthySodas

How to Make Healthy Sodas

The secret to nutritional, low-glycemic, tasty Kombucha sodas that are good for you!

by Dale H. Gillilan

Edited by Anne Louise Gillilan

"Healthy Sodas for Healthy Kids!"

Tools for the Journey

Dale Gillilan

Pécs, Hungary ◆ Kasilof, Alaska, USA

Copyright © 2018 by Dale H. Gillilan

Cover Design by Anne Louise Gillilan
Illustrations by Anne Louise Gillilan
Cover & Illustration Copyright © 2018 by Anne Louise
Gillilan

Disclaimer and Terms of Use: This book and all the information contained herein, including, but not limited to, the recipes and scientific information, are for educational and entertainment purposes only. They are not in any way to be construed as nutritional or medical advice or recommendation. If you have a medical condition, or seek nutritional or medical advice, go to an appropriate health care provider. While the information presented represents the understanding of the author, the author makes no claims regarding their scientific accuracy. In all things concerning your health and safety, you should do your "due diligence", meaning do your own research, seek appropriate expert advice, and make your own, informed decision. Only you (and, in consultation with your health care provider) can determine what is healthy for you. By using any of the information in this publication, you agree to assume full responsibility for your actions. With any lacto brewing method there is a chance of unhealthy or toxic bacteria infiltration. With any fermentation in sealed containers (as in the "secondary brew"), there is a possibility of bottles breaking under pressure, creating a serious risk to life and health. It is your responsibility to know the dangers, and to protect yourself from them if you choose to use any of the information in this publication. Again, this information is for educational and entertainment purposes only. Use at your own risk.

ISBN (print): 978-615-00-0238-5
ISBN (electronic): 978-615-00-0239-2

Printed in the United States of America and in the European Union

 http://ToolsForTheJourney.com

This book is dedicated to my best friend, my love and my companion – my wife – with special appreciation to our sons and daughter for their patience and feedback with all my experiments in "kitchen science."

"Let food be thy medicine and medicine be thy food."
attributed to Hippocrates

PREFACE

Lacto-brewing is truly an exciting and fun adventure for you, your family and friends. I want this book to provide the best possible introduction and guide to this wonderful world of healthy treats. And, I want people to know that there are inexpensive, smart, healthy alternatives to the health destroying refreshments that are commercially available. Will you help me on my crusade? Taking a few moments to make an honest review on Amazon can help others become healthier.

Because of the way that Amazon promotes books to others, five-star ratings are extremely important. A five-star rating will help make this book available to more people, so they, too, can benefit from creating their own healthy, nutritional soft drinks. Hopefully, you will be excited about this book and want it to be easily found by others, and will give it an honest five-star rating.

Likewise, your feedback provides important information to help me make meaningful updates to this book. if you have suggestions on how to improve it, or criticisms, I would like to hear from you. Please email me directly at:
Guide1@ToolsForTheJourney.com.

Thank you

HOW TO USE THIS BOOK

"How to Make Healthy Sodas" is a practical book about turning a major component of a national and international health disaster into a beneficial contributor to a healthy lifestyle. It is simultaneously a guidebook, a recipe book, a research manual, and a lab notebook.

Underlying all of the author's works is a philosophy of participatory education -- that the greatest advances in personal growth come through guided action. By creating a safe, structured and supportive experiential learning environment the student -- you, the reader -- is able to understand the principles of success. With this foundation, the student can shape their future path and use each success, or "failure", along the way to move them toward their goal.

This book gives the person interested in adding healthy refreshment to their diet the foundation, the tools, recipes and ideas to inspire creativity, and a structure to give the courage to develop new recipes.

The result is not a recipe book that is seldom used, but your book that is alive with your recipes that reflect your interests, tastes, health concerns and interests, and your needs. It becomes a reflection of your passions and your soul into the world in a vibrant, life-affirming and healthy way.

I have for you some additional resources that you will find beneficial as you delve into your natural sodas adventures. If you go to this website:
http://ToolsfortheJourney.com/2nd-brew-bonus, you can download a video that addresses questions about residual sugar and alcohol in Kombucha Tea. If you have any health issues that require monitoring your sugar intake, or if you are concerned about sugar in your diet for any reason, this will be helpful information. Likewise, if you have any issue with consuming alcohol, whether for sobriety, health, or other reasons, you will find this video informative.

In this video, I take you inside my kitchen laboratory where I dive into both of these issues and conduct experiments to find the answers for you. In the video, I also show you how I make Kombucha Tea, and how I do what is called a "continuous brew" that eliminates all the hassle of restarting your Kombucha brew every week. This is a simple, easy and very effective way I have been using for years. Our family loves it so much, I even hand carried the supplies to our home in Europe, so that we could continue making it the easy, efficient way there.

In addition to the video, you can download an infographic that shows the steps in an easy-to-follow fashion. This is ideal for use in the kitchen as you actually make your favorite Healthy Soda. You can print it in the size that is most convenient for you, and keep it handy as you brew up your new treat.

Are you ready? Grab your pencil; gather a few common kitchen tools; open this book and step into a new, healthier world -- let's bring flavorful, probiotic drinks into your life!

CONTENTS

Introduction   xv

Part I: How do we achieve such heavenly
dreams?   1

Chapter 1: What is Lacto-Brewing?   3

Chapter 2: What is Kombucha?   5

Chapter 3: Secondary Brew…
What does that mean?   9

Chapter 4: Flavors…Flavors…
Everywhere there are Flavors   10

Part II: How do I do this magic?   13

Chapter 5: What supplies do I need?   15

Chapter 6: Ok…That sounds a little strange…
Where do I get THAT?   26

Chapter 7: Got it…What are the steps?   29

Part III: I'm sold…Give me the recipes   33

Chapter 8: What are some basic recipes?   35

Chapter 9: I'm having fun now…
What else can I do?   42

Chapter 10: I've got my own recipes now!   62

Resources   71

About the Author   73

INTRODUCTION

Did you ever make root beer at home? When I was a child, my brother and I used to make it. It was a simple, fun process that used only a few simple ingredients, and produced a rich, creamy root beer that was far superior to anything purchased in a bottle or can. And, a root beer float made from your own root beer and homemade vanilla ice cream was the highlight of a summer party!

We gathered all the bottles we could from friends of the family: pop bottles and beer bottles that had the pry-off caps. Both types worked, but kids drinking out of beer bottles looked a little suspicious, so we avoided those if we could. The important thing was that they met two requirements: They had to withstand pressure, and they had to use pry-off lids.

While we were collecting the bottles, we saved our money to buy a bottle capper, and a box of bottle caps. The capper was a simple counter-top tool that sealed the bottles. When ready, you would place a cap on the bottle, set both under the capper and push the lever down. The capper would squeeze the cap around the lip of the bottle, creating (hopefully!) a tight seal.

The caps were much like the ones that were on the bottles originally. They were metal with a scalloped edge. They looked much like a tiny, metal upside-down bottom piecrust. Glued inside each cap was a round cork that functioned as the gasket to seal the bottle. In later years, these became a plastic seal.

Making the root beer was the fun part. After washing and sterilizing the bottles, we poured a five-pound bag of sugar (yes, it was a lot of sugar!) into a large pot, added a two-ounce bottle of wonderfully aromatic Hire's Root Beer Extract, then stirred in five gallons of warm water until it was all dissolved.

Of course, an occasional taste was required along the way. It tasted good, much like a commercial soda, but without the carbonation. But, the taste was nothing like what was coming in just a few days.

Finally, when the temperature was just right, we added the yeast. In those days, we used a cake of yeast. This was a moist square of yeast that needed to be refrigerated and used within a fairly short period of time after distribution from the producer. It was an active yeast, but not the "active, dry yeast" that we find in supermarkets today for use in bread making. The powdered yeasts of today do not produce the same result.

The bottles were filled, being careful to maintain the right amount of air in the bottle. They were then capped, and placed in an appropriate spot to "brew". This was usually in the bathtub. It needed to be a place that was warm and free of drafts. The bathtub was ideal because there was usually at least one bottle that "popped its cork" from too much pressure, and sprayed root beer everywhere! The bottles were placed on their sides to keep the cork moist; a towel was placed over them to keep spray to a minimum and to protect from drafts. Then, the long, difficult wait began....

It took anywhere from three to five days for the batch to "brew", or to carbonate. That seemed like years to a young boy. After about the third day, we would take a daily sample to see if it had reached perfection, yet. Once cooled in the refrigerator for a couple hours, we would open the bottle. We listened for the much-hoped-for pop, looked for the "head", or foam, and then hoped for the rich, creamy blend of root beer, sweetness, and slight yeasty taste. If all those elements were present to our liking (or, to the limit of our youthful patience), we loaded the refrigerator with bottles, and began our several weeks' pleasurable binge of root beers and root beer floats.

It is very difficult to find the supplies for that process today. While I have seen root beer extracts (and, other flavors) in specialty stores, they are not as flavorful as the old Hire's extract. Very recently, I discovered that Hire's drive-ins still sell their extract. This is the first time I have seen it in many years. I do not know if it is as good as it was in the past, but I do know the other brands I have tried are not as good. In my opinion, the other versions are not as rich and creamy. They seem sharper and more artificial tasting. The last store in my area to carry the yeast in cake form dropped it from their inventory a couple years ago. Powdered yeasts, even wine and champagne yeasts just don't work as well. The bottles are becoming a little rare to find. Twist-off caps, cans, and plastic bottles are much more common. And, then there are the cappers. They were once found in most hardware stores. I now only see them in beer brewing stores.

The real issue, though, is the health aspect. That was a lot of sugar! And, I don't know how natural the extract was. The main flavor we associate with the root beer taste comes from sassafras roots. These contain safrole, which the FDA has determined is a precursor to a carcinogen. Because of this, the sale of sassafras as a food additive was made illegal in the U. S. in 1960. As a result, all commercially available root beer drinks, and syrups for making root beer at home, use either an artificial sassafras flavor, or use an extract that has the safrole removed. With what you are learning here, you will be able to make healthy sodas that use all natural ingredients. You control the amount of sweetness, and you can use a low-glycemic sweetener that is much better for you than sugar. You can even make "medicinal" sodas – sodas that use herbs or foods that have healing qualities.

You might ask, "Nutritional" and "Soda" in the same sentence? Is it really possible? And, how about "sugar-free", or "low-glycemic", and "tasty"? Can this really be?

The answer is a resounding, "YES!" Not only that, but it is also very easy to make at home, and is very inexpensive. Are you tired of spending a dollar or more for a soda that is loaded with 37-52 grams of refined sugar in a 12-ounce (.35 L) drink?[1] According to the University of Nebraska, one teaspoon of sugar weighs four grams.[2] This amounts to 9-13 teaspoons of refined sugar in each drink! If you consume one soda each day, that amounts to about 65 POUNDS (29.5 kg) of sugar each year, which can add 15

---

[1] http://www.energyfiend.com/sugar-in-drinks
[2] http://lancaster.unl.edu/nep/thinkdrink.shtml

pounds (6.8 kg) of unnecessary weight to your body![3] This does not even consider the profound adverse health effects of caffeine, carbonic acid, artificial flavorings, and other ingredients.

Would you like to have a bubbly drink that has rich, natural flavor, tastes sweet, and can actually be healthy? Read on – this book will teach you how to make a natural soda in a variety of flavors…. Quickly…. Easily…. In your own kitchen.

Ready? Let's have some fun!

---

[3] http://lancaster.unl.edu/nep/thinkdrink.shtml

Part 1: How do we achieve such heavenly dreams?

CHAPTER 1: WHAT IS LACTO-BREWING?

Lacto-what??? What does that mean? Is this about making alcohol? Is it legal?

I can hear the questions now! And, the answers are simple. First, let me state that it is legal (as far as I know – you might want to make certain you don't live in some jurisdiction with a strange law….). You are **not** making alcoholic beverages. You are simply using naturally occurring yeasts to carbonate your recipe of teas, fruits, roots, and other flavorings. Let me explain what lacto-brewing is, and it will become clear to you.

Lacto-brewing is an ancient way of creating natural sodas and other foods. If the ingredients used are appropriate, the soda can be remarkably healthy. It is also used to make a variety of foods that you already know, such as yogurt, Kim-chi and sauerkraut (the real kind, not the chemically-made and rapidly-produced product on many grocery store shelves). There are others, however. You may have enjoyed sourdough pancakes, or sourdough bread before that is based on a "wild" yeast, or a commercial yeast. We frequently make pancakes and bread using a little KT as our "starter".

Lacto brewing, or lacto fermentation, is short for "lactic acid fermentation". It refers to process whereby cells (bacteria and yeast, in this case) convert sugars into energy and produce lactic acid as a byproduct.[4] In the muscles of our body, this is undesirable (remember the sore muscles from yesterday's over-exercising), but in the production of food, it can have some wonderful benefits.

Lactobacillus is the most common bacteria used, and is generally considered a beneficial probiotic that benefits the digestive tract. In this book we will be using what is known as Kombucha Tea, or as it is sometimes called "KT". This is a combination of yeasts and bacteria that live in a symbiotic culture. This means the yeast and bacteria work together for each other's benefit.

---

[4] http://en.wikipedia.org/wiki/Lactic_acid_fermentation

CHAPTER 2: WHAT IS KOMBUCHA?

I will only give a brief description of Kombucha, or "KT", here. (This book assumes you have a basic working knowledge of how to make KT. If you do not, or need a refresher, please watch our free video at http://ToolsfortheJourney.com/2nd-brew-bonus, or get our book, "Bright Line Eating Sodas".)

Kombucha Tea is a very old, with a number of stories about its history and origin. It is part of a large family of indigenous lacto fermentations that go back into antiquity. The Russians still make a fermented drink called Kvass from rye bread. Hungarians prepare a fermented pickle called Kovászos Uborka (literally, "leavened cucumbers", also called "sun pickles", or "sour pickles"). In Germany fruits are fermented in a rumtopf ("rum pot") to make a drink and preserved fruit. In Asia, you find foods like Kimchi, Natto, Tempeh, and more. Dairy products around the world are fermented in dishes like yogurt and kefir. Even some cheeses have historically depended upon the biological environments found in certain caves and cellars. Many cultures have fermented cabbage (sauerkraut), and lambic beers and wines. Even the ancient Egyptians had their lacto brew.

KT is actually a fascinating food. It is made from a "starter", which is a little bit of the "tea", or brew, that contains the cultures. To this is added a mixture of fresh-brewed tea and sugar. It is left to sit in a container that is covered by a breathable top; such as cheesecloth to keep dust, bugs and other things out until it tastes the way you like it. Simple!

The yeast converts the sugar to simple alcohol and carbonation. This carbonation is CO2 (carbon dioxide), which is used to create the "fizz", or carbonation, in commercial sodas. The bacteria feed off the alcohol and convert it into acetic acid. This is the main ingredient of vinegar. So, if you let it brew long enough it will end up tasting like a potent vinegar. This vinegary liquid has many health benefits, and can be used as a drink, for salads dressing, or most other places you would use vinegar. How far you allow your "brew" go towards a vinegary flavor is totally up to your personal tastes.

There are more factors that you can play with, such as the temperature, the sugar content, etc. However, it really is a virtually foolproof process as long as you follow some simple, basic rules and keep things clean. You mix the ingredients, and then take taste samples every day or two until it tastes the way you like.

To slow the process, just refrigerate the liquid. When it is at the taste level you want, pour off some of the "tea" and put it in the refrigerator. Be aware, it will not totally stop the yeast and bacterial processes, but will greatly slow them down. If you are drinking it within a few days to a couple weeks, the taste should not change noticeably. If it sits in your refrigerator for weeks or months, though, you will detect considerable changes in taste.

You do need to keep things clean, but a sterile lab environment is not required. Watch for the introduction of undesirable things, like molds, and all should go well. It is possible for your brew to go bad, but it does not happen often. In the 20-plus years I've been making KT,

I've only had a couple of batches go bad -- and, those were ones that I was using for more "adventurous", and unorthodox, experiments. Common sense goes a long way.

As part of the chemical and biological processes, the yeast and bacteria produce a cellulose matrix, called a SCOBY. This stands for "Symbiotic Colony of Bacteria and Yeasts." It is sometimes referred a "mushroom", although that is a nickname only. It has no biological relationship to a true fungus.

When you decant (pour off) some of the liquid from you KT to refrigerate, always keep some of the liquid and the SCOBY. These become the "starter" for your next batch. The SCOBY will grow over time. You only need to keep the top layer. This is the most recently developed layer, since it always grows a new SCOBY, or a new layer, at the top of the liquid.

Actually, you don't need the SCOBY at all. The bacteria and yeast are in the solution. I have brewed it many times without the SCOBY, it just takes a little longer.

In the free video, you are shown a simple method of making what is called a "continuous brew". This method is also described in my book, "Bright Line Eating Sodas". It is much simpler and does not require the weekly maintenance of the traditional method briefly described above. We have used it for years, and like it so much that I hand-carried a special jar to our home in Europe so we could use that process.

Don't worry…. that's the end of our chemistry lesson. This is not a course in the biochemistry of KT, nor is it a course in how to brew KT. I only wanted you to have a basic understanding, since we will be using KT as the basis for our sodas.

CHAPTER 3: SECONDARY BREW...WHAT DOES THAT MEAN?

There are actually two fermentation cycles (or, "brews") that we use. The first is the creation of Kombucha Tea, or KT, as discussed in Chapter 2. Once that process is completed to our satisfaction, we use the resulting KT to make our sodas. Since this, too, uses a natural fermentation process, or "lacto brew", to produce the carbonation, it is also called a "brew". And, since it is the second time we have fermented the liquid, it is called a "secondary brew".

Now that we have the definition, what does it really mean?

We will be taking our KT, adding a few wonderful ingredients to it, pouring it all into a bottle, capping it, and letting it sit in a warm place for a few days. Then, at the magical moment of perfection or, as close as our patience lets us wait, we will open it and fill our glass or mug with sparkling, heady, refreshing, natural soda.

The added ingredients are simple: various fruits and berries, a sweetener, and an occasional flavor enhancer. This might be something like cinnamon, ginger, or vanilla bean. In the next chapter, we'll talk more about flavors.

CHAPTER 4:
FLAVORS..FLAVORS...EVERYWHERE THERE ARE FLAVORS

The flavors you use are all around you. They're in your cupboard, on your counter, in your refrigerator, and in your grocery store. They can be simple, commonplace foods you frequently use. They can be exotic foods from faraway places. Or, something in between. You can use foods, or you can use prepared flavorings.

I prefer and recommend using real food. It works well, tastes wonderful, and you have the benefit of knowing the ingredients you put into your soda. Our motto is "Never buy foods with an ingredient list." We don't always manage to live up to that, but we come close. Whenever we have the time to prepare food from the basic ingredients, we do. I believe we end up with healthier food that way. This is just one more step in the path of eating healthy, while eating enjoyable foods.

So, what kind of flavors can you use?

Fruits are obvious. Look for fruits with lots of flavor. By this measure, lemon is a better choice than pear. There is probably a reason you don't see pear soda very often....

Berries are good, too. Most of the ones you would buy commercially are loaded with flavor: blueberries, blackberries, currants, etc.

You can use dried fruits and berries. I do that all the time. However, they do produce a different flavor than fresh or frozen fruit. You will have to try them all to see what you like best. Speaking of frozen fruits and berries – they work really well. They seem to give lots of carbonation, too. So, if you like sodas with "head" (foam), try some frozen ingredients.

Fruit juices can be used, too. Again, pick the more flavorful ones. There is also a difference between fresh juices, and concentrates. Try making a grape soda with grape juice, then make it with frozen grape juice concentrate. The concentrate will give a stronger flavor without diluting the KT as much.

You can use some herbs and spices. Vanilla, ginger, and cinnamon are examples. Herbs, and especially, spices are often used to enhance a fruity flavor. One of our favorites is cranberry cinnamon soda. The cinnamon gives it a little extra punch that complements the cranberries nicely. You can use things like mulling spices, even shredded coconut works well. Chocolate, or carob, can be an interesting additive.

Be willing to experiment. You are making this one bottle at a time, so the risk of an "undesirable" recipe is very small. It is by experimenting that we have discovered our family favorites. And, those favorites change often as we discover some new flavor idea that turns out wonderfully delicious and appealing. In fact, there have been very few attempts that were disasters, if any. It seems to be really hard to make one that doesn't taste at least good.

This book is an introduction to healthy sodas, and its intention is to get you started making them. So, I'm only

going to mention one other aspect of healthy sodas –
"medicinal" sodas. Using the word "medicinal" may not
be appropriate, actually (although, I understand that in
the "olden days", patent medicines were often mixed in
soda-like drinks).   I'm definitely not recommending
making sodas out of any kind of medicine. What I am
referring to, is using as flavorings the herbs, foods and
other natural substances that have identified healing
properties. These can then be consumed as a healthy,
flavorful soda that has the added benefit of providing the
healing properties that are being sought. Using this idea,
we recently made a honey-garlic soda. We have also
added gobo (burdock root) to some of our sodas. In short,
anything that you could make into a tea or tincture, you
could consider for a soda. There are other factors to
consider as well, but this will get you thinking creatively.
And, thinking creatively is what will help you find the
"perfect" soda for you.

Part III: How do I do this magic?

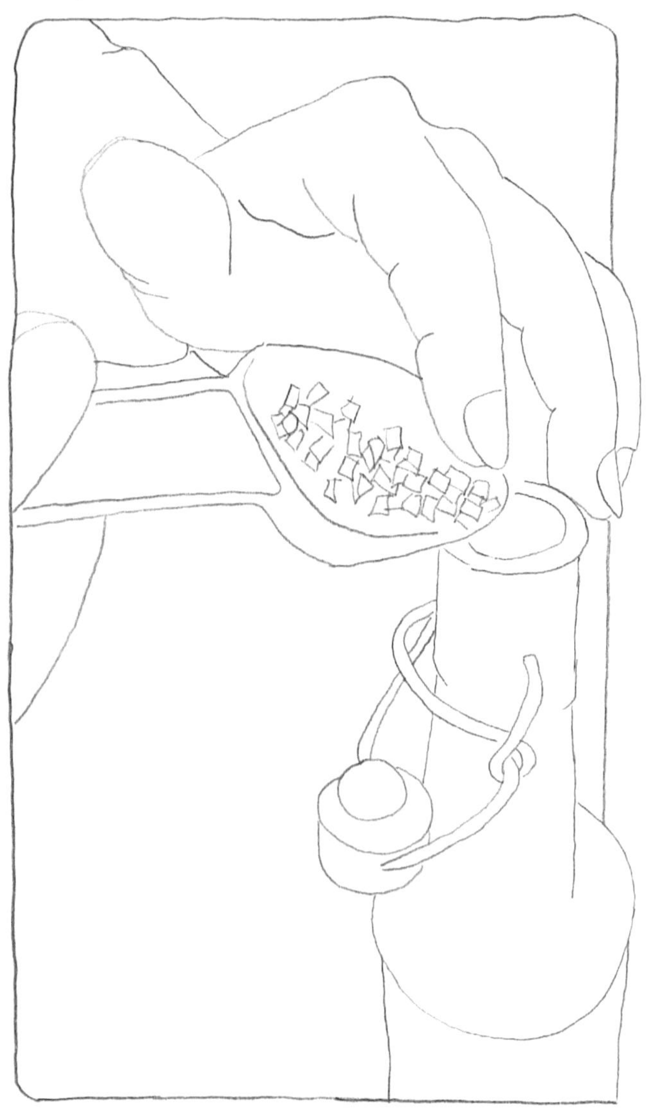

CHAPTER 5: WHAT SUPPLIES DO I NEED?

Your supplies fall into four categories:

- Kitchen tools and implements
- Flavorings and sweetener
- Kombucha Tea (KT)
- Bottles

Kitchen tools and implements

The kitchen tools and implements are easy. The main thing to remember is to avoid metal if at all possible. Stainless steel is ok, but is best avoided. The acetic and other acids (vinegar) in the KT can react with the metal. Realistically, this is probably not an issue because of the short time it is in the container, but I like to use glass, wood, or plastic instead.

You need a measuring cup. This is more for pouring than measuring. You could use a funnel, instead. But you still need a container for the KT once you get it from your KT jar, until you pour it into your secondary brew bottle.

A heavy towel is good for covering the filled bottles while they are fermenting and carbonating. This helps insulate them for maintaining consistent temperature, reduces the effects of drafts, and prevents problems if a bottle leaks or breaks.

Flavorings and sweeteners

The flavorings we have talked about. Pick a simple, strong flavor for your first batch. They give encouraging results.

The sweetener I use is agave syrup. It is sweeter tasting than sugar, so it takes less. It is low-glycemic, so it does not create the sugar spikes and crashes. This also makes it possibly better for people with insulin issues (check with your doctor if that is your issue).

Honey can be used, but it is generally not recommended for the KT, because it has anti-biotic qualities, which tend to kill of the yeast and bacteria. I have experimented with it some, and have had success using it. You might want to experiment on your own before you make your judgement about honey.

Sugar can be used, although I personally would not recommend it, because of the effects it has on the body. I do use organic cane juice in my KT, but that also gets converted into other ingredients in the KT brewing process.

I have not tried stevia. I suspect it would not work, though. I do not believe it will provide the nutrients for the yeast. You would probably end up with a sweet drink with little or no carbonation.

Bottles

The types of bottles you use are critical for proper brewing, and for safety. Let's discuss the safety issue in detail. It may sound scary, but like many things in life, you need to use common sense and have respect for the processes involved. That, coupled with appropriate knowledge, will serve you well.

If you have done everything correctly, and if all the conditions are right for the yeast to do its "magic", then you will have a carbonated soda when it is all done. By definition, this means the liquid inside the bottle will be under pressure. This pressure can become strong enough to break a bottle that is not designed for the produced pressure. In an extreme situation, it could explode violently, sending glass shards and sticky solution everywhere.

In all my years of brewing, I have only had a few bottles break. None have been explosive, like I just described. Here are the factors that will help you prevent a disaster:

➢ Use ONLY bottles that are designed to hold pressure. This could include champagne bottles, most wine bottles, beer bottles and soda bottles.

    ➢ The proper bottles will have a concave (indented) bottom. If you're not sure what that means, look at a champagne bottle, and notice how much the bottom of the bottle curves inward. That inward curve is a characteristic of what is called a "pressure vessel". It helps the bottle to withstand the pressure inside it.

    ➢ The proper bottles will be round, never square. I made this mistake once and used a square juice bottle with a wire bale and stopper. The bottle cracked, and the bottom came off.

    ➢ Beer bottles with wire bales and stoppers are the best, in my opinion. I have never had one break. I have had them leak, which I consider to be a wonderful safety feature. What that means is that the wire bale acted like a spring that gently gave when the pressure became too great, thus releasing the excess pressure and then resealing once the pressure was again under control. When I made root beer as a child, the caps we used generally made a very tight seal, and if the pressure became too great, the bottle would break. These type of beer bottles are generally heavier (thicker) than soda bottles, adding to their safety.

    ➢ Some people use plastic 1 or 2-liter soda bottles. These do have the advantage in that you can squeeze them and get a good sense of how pressurized (carbonated) your drink is. I have never had one of these break, despite being highly carbonated. If it did break, you would avoid the issue of glass shards. The major drawback to using plastic bottles, is the possibility of leaching chemicals out of the plastic, which many health-conscious people are concerned about today.

> Cover your bottles with a heavy towel while they are fermenting. It is traditional to lay them on their side, although that is not absolutely necessary. It was done historically so that the cork would stay moist and create a better seal. Bottles with ceramic tops, plastic tops or plastic lined tops do not have that requirement. The other reason to keep them horizontal is to expose a larger surface of solution (your soda) to the air, to help the fermentation process. Whether you stand them up, or place them horizontally, putting a towel over them will help contain any disasters and avoid drafts.

> Use some precautions when you open the bottle. If you are using the beer bottles with the wire bail, I suggest keeping one hand on top of the stopper when you pop the bail. And, push down firmly, especially if your recipe has a history of being highly carbonated! I learned this the hard way. I opened a bottle one time with both thumbs pushing on the bail. When the bail released, the stopper and bail slipped off the bottle and went flying. I was holding it over the kitchen sink at the time, and barely missed hitting the window above the sink! I have no doubt it would have broken the window. As it was, I only had to clean up the soda that sprayed all over the window and cabinets. With my hand holding firmly on top of the stopper, the worst that happens is I get a lot of foam running over my hands and the bottle. Sometimes, I will also place a

towel or cloth over the stopper as I open it. This helps localize any possible spray that might sneak past the cap and your hand.

Kombucha Tea (KT)

You will need a supply of Kombucha Tea, or KT. You might find a friend or neighbor who is willing to share some with you, but your best bet is to make it yourself. It is simple to make, and a healthy drink itself.   It requires tea, water, sugar and a "starter".

I first made KT about 25 years ago. At that time, it was a hassle, even in its simplicity. It required two large jars as fermenting vessels (ours were one gallon each). When one was "ready" (i.e., it had reached the level of acidity – vinegar taste- that we could tolerate), we placed it in the refrigerator. We drank from it while the second one brewed on the counter.

It was actually quite a process to prepare the first jar for drinking, and the second for brewing. When the first batch was done brewing, we removed the SCOBY, setting it on a clean plate or bowl. Then we decanted (removed) the liquid from the jar by pouring or using a ladle, and putting it into another jar that went into the refrigerator. We kept a small amount of the liquid aside to add to the next batch as a "kick-starter".

Next, we turned our attention to the new batch. We scrubbed out the jar, rinsed it very thoroughly so that no soap residue remained. We dried the jar thoroughly to remove any traces of chlorine from the water, which might kill the good bacteria and yeast. We wiped the inside of the jar with white distilled vinegar. This acted as to remove any stray "nasties", like bacteria that might have been on our hands or the towel, and created an acidic environment to support our fermentation culture.

After preparing our new mixture by cooking tea and sugar, then allowing them to cool properly, we refilled the jar with the mixture. While the mixture was cooling, we separated the "mother" SCOBY (the original one) from the new "daughter" SCOBY. We discarded the "mother" SCOBY and used the 'daughter" SCOBY in the next batch. We stirred in the KT we had set aside from the prior batch as a "starter", set the daughter SCOBY in, covered the mouth of the jar with cheesecloth, and set the jar aside for its week of brewing.

When the second batch was done, and assuming the first jar was empty, the process began again. It was a lot of work! Because it was so much work, I stopped making it for a while after we moved to a new home.

Besides being a lot of work, the finished drink was much less palatable. We always used simple black tea and white sugar. Those seemed to be the ingredients everyone used at the time. And, we brewed it until it tasted much like vinegar. In fact, it was much like drinking vinegar, or diluted vinegar. Ugh! It seemed no one had heard of secondary brew, or of using other teas. Today, we use a variety of teas, each producing a different flavored KT. One of our favorites is to use an organic green jasmine tea. It produces a fruity tasting

KT with a hint of apple cider. To avoid contamination from pesticides and other nasty things, it is always best to use certified organic teas from known, reliable sources.

I am also glad to report that the process has evolved into something much simpler. That simplicity has enabled me to enthusiastically make KT for many years now. What's the secret?

I now use a continuous brew process for the primary fermentation. Simply put this means as I remove KT from my jar, I replace it. One day's drinking KT is taken out, and it is replaced with the same amount of sweetened tea solution. In that way, it is constantly producing KT that tastes the way I want it.

You can do this by pouring off, or ladling off some KT. But there is an easier solution. Sun Tea jars! These are the one gallon jars that have a spout on them. You drain off what you want to drink, then once each day, you top it off. Periodically you need to remove some of the SCOBY's, and clean out the jar. But this is a job that is done once every month or two, not weekly.

We keep three batches of KT going, rotating them each day. So, one gets used, then sits for two days before it is used again. Each night we prepare a batch of fresh tea with organic dried cane juice ("sugar") to add to tomorrow's KT. This is usually 1 or 1-1/2 liter of fresh tea. We prepare it, filter out the leaves, then pour it in the gallon jar. It sits overnight, and is ready to drink in the morning of the third day.

This system of "one day on; two days off" seems to make a very nice drink for us. Experiment with it. You may like something that has brewed longer (giving it a more vinegar-like taste), or shorter (making it taste sweeter). Also, if you consume more than we do, you may need it to sit longer before it is used again, because the ratio of fresh sugar is being changed more aggressively. The opposite is true if you consume less. For example, if you only drink a cup a day, and you will probably want to use only one or two gallon jars for your system. Otherwise, it will probably become much too strong in a few weeks.

Another option is to decant, or drain off, more KT from your jar. This becomes wasteful, though, unless you have some uses for the KT. If you wish to do this, do a little research on the websites listed below. There are many viable uses for KT. Some people swear by it as a hair conditioner. Some feed it to their plants and, compost the SCOBY's. Some use it much like vinegar. Dogs usually love to chew the SCOBY's, and the liquid is said to reduces itching. There are many available recipes for all parts of your wonderful lacto-brew. I will soon be releasing a book that details how to make your own delicious probiotic KT, with explanations of a very easy way to streamline the process. This method minimizes the time you spend preparing your KT, which means you are more likely to make this wonderful drink a part of your daily diet. You can, also, easily find basic recipes by doing a quick search on internet. If you would like to be informed of the release of my new book, you can sign up at: http://ToolsfortheJourney.com/subscribe.

Oh, in case you are wondering…. The teas we use to make our KT are green jasmine, Darjeeling, and gunpowder green tea. Sometimes we use Pu-er, but it is a little harder to locate where we live. We only use organic tea, and we buy it in bulk. The quality of tea, and thus the KT, is far superior with bulk organic teas. Using the three-jar rotation method just described, a pound of tea will last about a year for us.

If you look around, you can find wholesalers who will sell it in one-pound bags at very reasonable prices. Starwest Botanicals, http://www.starwest-botanicals.com, is one source we use. You can talk to your local health food store, or even your local grocer, about a bulk order. They will often make very appealing arrangements on bulk purchases. Although you can buy tea in most grocery stores, it pays to get a high quality, organic tea. There is a tremendous flavor difference, as well as the added health benefits. While small quantities of organic tea may be more expensive, the organic teas become very price competitive when you buy in bulk.

There are places that sell some specialized, or exotic, teas. Pu-er is an example. If you live in an area with a large Chinese population that supports an Oriental shopping district (like Seattle, San Francisco, Philadelphia, etc.), then you can easily find Pu-er. You can also buy it from companies like The Happy Herbalist, http://www.happyherbalist.com. Another good place to find specialty teas is teas shops or teas houses. We have even found Pu-er in small European towns that have a tea shop. Be certain, though, that it is pure tea, not tea with an aromatic oil added like Earl Grey. Those oils can interfere with the brewing process.

But, it all starts with the SCOBY and some "starter", so let's talk about that.

CHAPTER 6: OK...THAT SOUNDS A LITTLE STRANGE...WHERE DO I GET *THAT?*

There are a number of places to get SCOBY's and "starter" (sometimes called a "mother"). The first place to look is among your friends. Ask around. You may already know someone who is brewing Kombucha Tea. If so, ask for a starter. They will be happy to provide you with one. I have yet to meet a KT brewer who is not eager to share their prize. They are constantly "growing" new SCOBY's, and few have any use for them. Add a little KT liquid, into a zip-lock bag or a glass jar (remember…avoid a metal lid) along with the SCOBY and you have a starter to take home.

Kombucha is much more popular now than it was 25 years ago, but maybe you are the "fringe" element among your friends and associates, and none of them have even heard of KT. You don't know anyone with an extra SCOBY, what now? I'd suggest putting an ad on Craig's list, www.craigslist.com, on Facebook, or on Freecycle. Freecycle is found by going to https://www.freecycle.org, then searching for the names of your nearby communities. It is also found on Facebook at https://www.facebook.com/freecycle. The rules for Freecycle are that you may ask for or advertise things that are free. No bartering. No selling. Free only. The idea is to keep useful things out of the landfill, and to help one another. When I checked, there were 10,427 local Freecycle groups, so there are good chances of finding one near you. You can also frequently find various groups on Facebook that are oriented toward selling, bartering, or giving away items of all kinds. You can also find groups that are centered around dieting, lifestyle, healthy foods and similar interests, that can be helpful. Be certain to get on your local version of each of these.

There used to be a world-wide clearing house for exchange of KT starters. The exchange has ended, but the owner still offers to send starters worldwide for the cost of the postage, http://www.kombu.de/suche2.htm

If you cannot find a free local source, you can always buy one. There are several online sources. If you have trouble locating a source, look in the Resources section of this book.

You can even find them for sale on Amazon, https://www.amazon.com/.

There is one other way to get a "starter". Buy a bottle of KT from your local health foods store, or the health food section of your local grocery store. **Be absolutely certain it has not been pasteurized, however.** That would destroy the culture. In my opinion, this is much like buying plain yogurt to use to start your own yogurt batch. In both cases you want the plain product (no added flavors, preservatives or chemicals), and you want it unpasteurized. I have not tried this method, but I have repeatedly started a new batch using just the liquid as the starter without a SCOBY.

In the "early days" of making KT we all believed that you needed the SCOBY to start a new batch. But, now we understand the SCOBY is just the cellulose structure that is built for, and by, the bacteria and yeast, and they exist throughout the liquid. That's why this method can work.

By the way, if you have been buying bottles of KT at a store, you have a pleasant surprise ahead of you. You should be able to make several gallons of fresh KT for the price of one store-bought bottle. And, the flavor will be much better -- it will be just the way **you** like it!

CHAPTER 7: GOT IT...WHAT ARE THE STEPS?

The process is really very simple. Once you have the KT with just the right amount of tartness, you add your flavoring ingredients some additional sweetener, bottle and cap it, then set it in a warm place to ferment for a couple more days.

I should share a note about the flavor of the KT. It is okay for it to be a little "dry" or vinegary tasting. It will become more flavorful during the secondary brew.

Sometimes you will get "ooglies" in your brew. These are small strands of a developing SCOBY. Some people just drink them down. Others prefer to filter them out. If you want to filter them, you can use a tea filter, tea ball, coarse sieve, etc.

Here are the details.

General procedure:

1. Be certain the bottle is thoroughly cleaned and sterilized (if you choose to sterilize).

2. The steps can be done in any order, but I recommend adding the KT last so that you can control the headspace (air at the top of the bottle) better.

3. Cut (if necessary) and measure the flavoring: fruit, juice, roots, etc. Just be sure to keep the pieces small, so you can get them out of the bottle easily.

4. Put the flavoring in the bottle. Use whatever means seems appropriate. If it's liquid, pour it in. For solids you may pour them, or place them in with your fingers (you DID clean your hands, didn't you?)

5. Add the sweetener of your choice. In these recipes, we use agave syrup. With other sweeteners, you may need to experiment to find the best ratio. It **is** important to use natural sweeteners that contain some form of sugar. Artificial sweeteners, and sugar substitutes, like stevia, do not provide the "fuel" for the yeast to produce the carbonation.

6. Pour the KT into the bottle stopping at the appropriate level. You should keep 1-1 ½" (25-38mm)· headspace (air) at the top of the bottle. You may need to experiment with this to find the ideal space for your tastes and environment. The flavoring and sweetener you use can also affect the amount of headspace needed to get a good carbonation of the finished soda.

7. Cap the bottle. Check the seal by tipping the bottle. If it leaks, open it and reseal, then repeat the test. If it is sealed properly (the wire bale snapped down), it should not leak.

   If it does, check the rubber gasket. They can be reused MANY times, but they do eventually fail. Replace the gasket if necessary. You can usually buy more gaskets at stores that sell home brewing supplies for making beer and wine. Of course, this is assuming you are using the beer bottles with the wire bail and ceramic stopper.

   Whatever you are using, check for leaks. If you are using a capper, and it leaks, you will need to remove the cap and use a new one. If it is a plastic soda bottle, make certain the lid is screwed on tight. If it still leaks, try a different cap, or replace the bottle and cap. Plastic wrap under the cap might help achieve a tighter seal as well.

8. Place the bottle in a warm place free from drafts and at a fairly constant temperature. You may need to experiment with the temperature. I have brewed it on our kitchen countertop, alongside the KT.

    In the winter, it can get into the mid-sixties (17-19°C) at night in our kitchen, so it might take an extra day to finish. Most of the time I put it in our utility room. This is where the water heater and furnace are, so it stays fairly warm in there, especially in the wintertime. You need to be careful to avoid too much heat. In the utility room, I place the bottles in a plastic box on a chair so it is a little lower and the temperature seems about perfect – probably in the mid-seventies. Cover or wrap in a towel.

9. When you think it is done, after two days is a good start, put it in the refrigerator. After it is thoroughly cool, pop it open. I would recommend doing this outside until you get this figured out. If it set too long, or carbonated too much, it can create a huge spray. It is kind of like a liquid Roman Candle fireworks! No flames, of course… and, no fire hazard… just a big mess if it gets on your walls! Oh… and, be certain to point it away from any person, pet, or anything breakable… (Are you scared, yet? Don't be… just be safe and smart.)

As I mentioned before, I always hold one hand over the top of the stopper when I pop the bail (the wire that holds the stopper in place). That way, if it is over carbonated, I can slowly release the pressure, instead of having a "rogue fountain". I now open the bottles over the sink.

If you want more carbonation, simple replace the stopper, and return it to its brewing location. You might also try adding more sweetener.

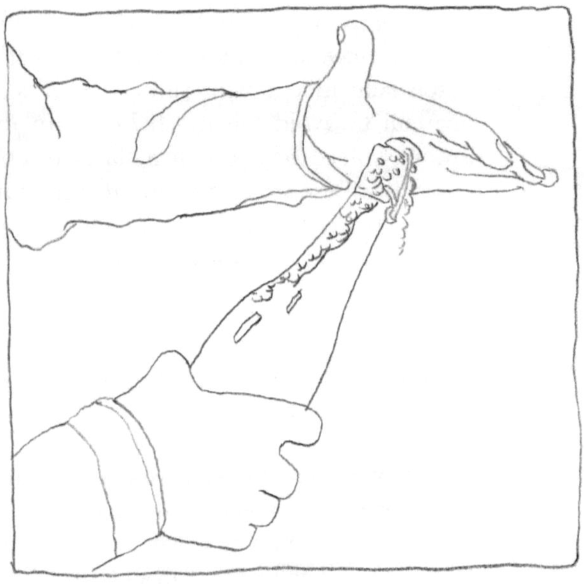

Part IIII: I'm sold...Give me the recipes

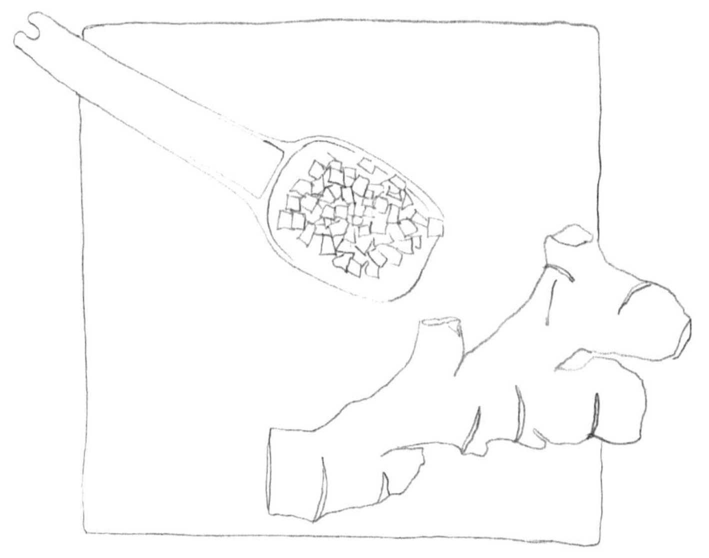

CHAPTER 8: WHAT ARE SOME BASIC RECIPES?

Here are some recipes to get you started. While these might be called "basic", their taste is exquisite. There are enough here to give you a good understanding of how easy it is to create delicious, healthy sodas. From here, you can begin to experiment on your own. Remember, very little can go wrong, and there are no mistakes – just adventures!

If you want to explore more "adventurous" or more "exotic" recipes, or recipes that some use as herbal remedies, go to our website, http://ToolsfortheJourney.com/subscribe, and sign up to be notified when our next book is published.

Lime Rickey (option A)

Have you ever had a Lime Rickey? We used to buy them at Arctic Circle drive-ins (when we lived near them and still ate fast food). They were wonderfully refreshing on a hot summer day. These versions are equally refreshing, but much healthier.

½ cup grape juice

1 t concentrated lime juice

3 t agave syrup

Darjeeling KT (or, whatever type you like)

This produces a gentle grape taste with the lime twist. Carbonation is moderate with a light head and a light, bubbly taste.

Lime Rickey (option B)

Grape juice concentrate (we use frozen grape juice concentrate)

Juice squeezed from a fresh lime

Your favorite KT

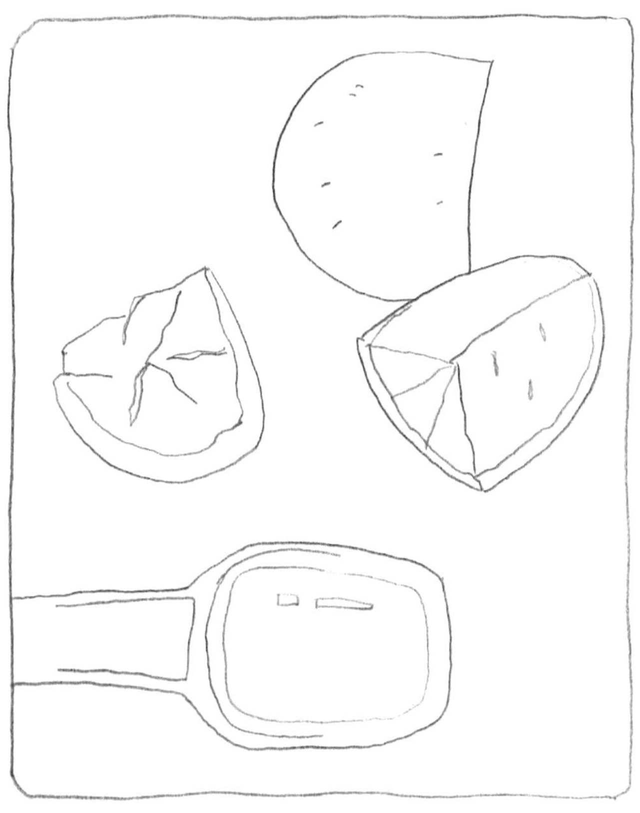

Lemon-Ginger Soda, aka "The World's Best Lemonade"

This is an amazing carbonated lemonade. If you like lemonade, you will want to drink this by the gallons!

¾ T diced fresh ginger

Fresh lemon: slice in half and squeeze enough to make about 2 T of juice

About ¼ of the lemon rind (about 1T) as a zest. Be certain to cut or tear the rind into small pieces. They will expand during the fermentation period.

2-3 t agave syrup

We use Gunpowder Green Tea KT. What will you use?

Some people like it drier. If that fits your tastes, then use the lesser amount of sweetener.

This recipe is a lightly carbonated drink – perfect for those who prefer a "softer" drink.

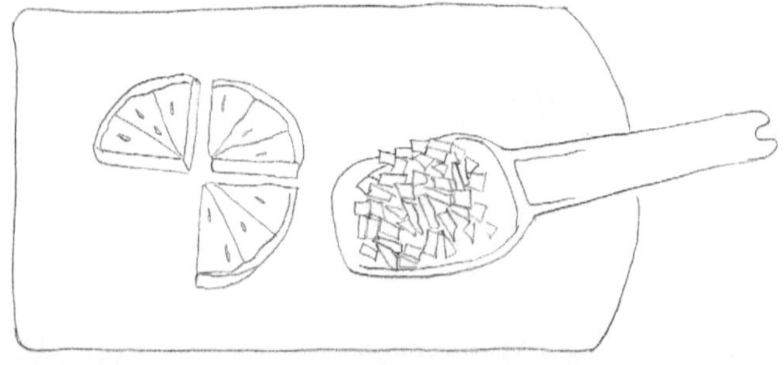

Cherry-Berry Soda

¼ cup fresh or frozen berries and cherries

2 T agave syrup

Your favorite KT

Cut or tear the cherries into small strips (about 1/8"-1/4", or 6-8mm, wide). Unless the berries are very large, they should be fine whole. If they are large, cut or tear them as well. This is very good with dark cluster berries, such as blackberries and Marion berries.

Mixed Berry Delight

2 heaping T dried berries (we used blueberries, strawberries and cherries)

2 T agave syrup

Green Jasmine KT is a nice blend for this recipe

A fun part of using fruit is to leave the fruit in the soda when you serve it. The pieces are bubbly on the tongue and flavorful!

Any recipe I have used that include fresh or frozen berries tends to be **very** carbonated. It creates a great, frothy head! However, you need to be careful opening the bottle. It tends to foam out dramatically! As I've said before, open it over a sink, and keep your hand on the top, so you can ease the pressure off.

Natural Cream Soda

Cream soda makes a nice float with homemade ice cream.

¼ t pure vanilla extract

2 T agave syrup

Darjeeling KT

CHAPTER 9: I'M HAVING FUN NOW...WHAT ELSE CAN I DO?

In a word: "Experiment!"

The long version: "Have Fun!"

The easiest way to experiment is to play with flavors. As I said before, fruits and spices are probably the first place to start. What is your favorite fruit or fruit combination? Try it in a secondary brew!

Do you have favorite spices you like with fruits? You might like cinnamon with apples, applesauce, apple juice or apple cider. If so, then try a secondary brew with some apple juice, or apple slices and cinnamon bark, or ground cinnamon.

Perhaps you like spiced peaches. Then try some peach slices with a few cloves in your secondary brew.

Do you enjoy the warm taste of mulled wine? Get some mulling spices (or, make some from a recipe), add them to grape juice and put them in your secondary brew.

Then, you might try dried fruit, fresh fruit and fruit juices. The taste of each is different. Just be sure to keep the pieces small, so you can get them out of the bottle easily.

Once you've gained some confidence with fruit, you can expand to flavors. Vanilla extract, or vanilla bean, is a natural choice. But, don't stop there. What about some shredded coconut? Or, get some root beer extract (or, a root beer recipe), and make a healthy root beer.

And, don't forget the vegetables and herbs… I once tasted celery soda (great with a light lunch!). I have put Gobo (burdock root) in my sodas. This is often used as a purifying agent, and tasted very good in the soda. If you need to take an herb on a regular basis, this is one way to do it and to make it enjoyable. Just make certain that the other ingredients are appropriate for your condition.

My caution is to be smart about what you use. Make certain that the ingredients are appropriate to ferment, and that they are appropriate for your body and needs. If you do that, you are at the beginning of a fun and flavorful adventure!

The following are pages with blank forms so that you can record your "kitchen science" experiments. I suggest recording both successes, and ones that did not turn out to your liking. Having that record will help you in the future as you consider other ideas for ingredients. It will also help you identify other aspects, besides the ingredients that may have affected your success. All of this information will be valuable to you in the future.

Your notes can take whatever form is appropriate and meaningful for you. You might find that a photograph, or a drawing, communicates an important aspect very succinctly. If so, add them. Make the experiment records and the recipes yours. Make them meaningful, memorable, and have fun!

Once you have identified a combination of ingredients and process that you like, you can add it to the "My Recipes" section in Chapter 10.

If you are reading this as an eBook, it is only slightly different. Since you cannot enter data into most eBooks, I have included one page of the *"Kitchen Science" Experiment Records*, and one page of the *"My Recipes"* entry. You may then use these as patterns to use in a notebook, or some other appropriate location. In addition, you may obtain a free copy of both the *"Kitchen Science" Experiment Record"* and the *"My Recipes"* entry from our website. These are pdf's in a variety of sizes, both US and European. Just download them, print off the size you want in the quantity you want, and put them into an appropriate book. You can get these at http://ToolsfortheJourney.com/2nd-brew-bonus.

Before you begin, let me explain a couple parts of each entry that might not be readily apparent.

"Environmental conditions and temperature:"

This where you describe the ambient conditions while the secondary brew was happening. Temperature will radically affect the fermentation, but so can other variables. If it is summer time with the windows open and a thunderstorm comes through that creates strong drafts and cools the room ten degrees for several hours, your fermentation will be impacted. If it is winter and you put the bottles in the oven with the light on for heat, your results may be very different from a batch that is left on the counter overnight.

"Ingredients;"

Be accurate here. This helps to make it repeatable so that it becomes a reliable recipe. If you add lemon juice, how much did you add? Be specific, either by volume measure, or by weight. Likewise, let's say you add an ingredient, cayenne for example, and it is too strong, you try it again with a lesser amount, and it is too weak. If you have recorded the ingredients accurately, you can narrow down to the exact amount that will give the flavor you are expecting and seeking.

"Special procedures, or other considerations:"

This is a catch-all for anything else that might have an effect upon the experiment, and the observed impact. It could include things like:

- Did you provide any sustained, or intermittent, heat for the bottles?

- Did you decide to mix all the ingredients in a bowl and then pour them into the bottle, rather than putting each ingredient into the bottle individually?

- Did you play music with a speaker next to the bottles, pre-heat the bottles, or any other unusual consideration that you want to evaluate?

"Bottle type used:"

Are you using beer bottles with wire bales? Screw-top wine bottles? Soda or beer bottles with caps? Plastic soda bottles? The bottle can be an important consideration in how much pressure it obtains (which is a factor in carbonation). You might also want to know if there are any impacts of flavor, any leakage, etc.

"Headspace allowed:"

How full you make each bottle is an important part of the carbonation. Too much, or too little, and you will not have the desired carbonation. You are seeking a perfect balance of headspace, temperature, brewing time, and sugar content, so each should be recorded.

"KT type and description:"

What is the tea you used? What kind of sugar? Did you change anything in the KT? Even the brand of tea can radically alter the taste. I have used Jasmine Green tea for one of my KT brews for many years. Recently, I had to purchase a different brand of Jasmine Green tea. There was a radical taste difference. The new brand has significantly more jasmine in it. So much more, that the KT no longer tastes like a slightly fruity, tangy KT. Instead, it has a strong, flower-like taste. That one change would significantly alter the flavor profile of a secondary brew.

The description is anything that might be useful to you in evaluating, comparing and replicating this experiment as another experiment, or as a recipe. For example, you might want to document the taste of the KT. Is it sweet, acidic ("vinegary"), or a "sweet-sour" mix? You might want to document your assessment based upon your "calibrated tongue". Or, you can get more scientific and use litmus paper ("pH strips") or other instruments to measure the acidity of your KT. You could also use a Brix hygrometer to measure sugar content. It's all up to you. But, decide what is important for you without creating overwhelm, and record it!

One other consideration that fits under the "description" category is the age of your KT. By this I do not mean the age of that batch. Rather, I am talking about how long you have been brewing that KT in that location. If you have two different batches of KT brewing that came from two different sources, they could very well taste quite different. This is because they probably have different strains of bacteria and yeast, which will affect the final chemical composition and the taste.

The yeast and bacteria that are naturally within any location will change the biological composition and profile of your KT over time. This means that if you have a KT brew that you have maintained for several years in your urban apartment, and another one that is just as old and came from the same "starter" that you keep in your weekend cabin by the lake, they can develop different tastes. That happens because the local bacteria and yeast are slowly entering into and affecting your KT. This is one of the characteristics of what is called "lambic" fermentation.

"Duration of secondary brew:"

This is simply a record of how long you left the bottles to ferment. It will usually be measured in hours.

"Other information:"

This is a space for anything else you want to track and record that might be meaningful to you. It could even be a record of one-off events that might help you evaluate results. For example, you might have mixed all your ingredients in a bowl, then were called away for three hours before you could fill and cap the bottles. That would be a note that could be valuable in assessing the results.

"Results:"

This is an **objective** evaluation of the outcome of this particular secondary brew. You can make it as scientific and precise as you wish and are able. For example, if you have a Brix hygrometer, you might record the residual (remaining) sugar content to give you a precise measure of sweetness.

"My personal evaluation:"

This is where you make your own **subjective** assessment, or those of others who are acting as your test subjects. You might comment on appearance, head (foam), carbonation, taste, bouquet (smell), aftertaste, etc.

The important message about this document is that you should not rely upon memory to keep track of how you did something. Our memories are imperfect, and important details can be lost over time. Besides, when you get that perfect soda that your family loves, it would be a shame to have it lost because you neglected to document how to make it.

THIS PAGE LEFT INTENTIONALLY BLANK

Date:_________________   Time:_________________

Environmental conditions and temperature:___________

____

____

____

____

Ingredients:____

____

____

____

____

____

____

____

____

Special procedures, or other considerations:___________

____

____

____

____

Bottle type used:___________________________________

____

____

Headspace allowed:_________________________________

KT type and description:_____________________________

____

____

Duration of secondary:_______________________________

____

____

Other information:_______________________________________

____

____

____

____

Results:____

____

____

____

____

My personal evaluation:_________________________________

____

____

____

____

____

____

____

____

____

____

____

____

Date:_________________   Time:_______________

Environmental conditions and temperature:___________

____

____

____

____

Ingredients:______________________________________

____

____

____

____

____

____

____

____

Special procedures, or other considerations:___________

____

____

____

____

Bottle type used:_________________________________

____

____

Headspace allowed:_______________________________

KT type and description:___________________________

____

____

Duration of secondary:_______________________________

____

____

Other information:_________________________________

____

____

____

____

Results:____

____

____

____

____

My personal evaluation:_____________________________

____

____

____

____

____

____

____

____

____

____

____

____

____

Date:___________________   Time:___________________

Environmental conditions and temperature:___________

____

____

____

____

Ingredients:_____________________________________

____

____

____

____

____

____

____

____

Special procedures, or other considerations:___________

____

____

____

____

Bottle type used:_________________________________

____

____

Headspace allowed:_______________________________

KT type and description:____________________________

____

____

Duration of secondary:_______________________________

____

____

Other information:_______________________________________

____

____

____

____

Results:____

____

____

____

My personal evaluation:___________________________________

____

____

____

____

____

____

____

____

____

____

____

____

____

Date:______________________   Time:______________________

Environmental conditions and temperature:____________

____

____

____

____

Ingredients:______________________________________

____

____

____

____

____

____

____

____

Special procedures, or other considerations:____________

____

____

____

____

Bottle type used:__________________________________

____

____

Headspace allowed:________________________________

KT type and description:_____________________________

____

____

Duration of secondary:______________________________

____

____

Other information:_________________________________

____

____

____

____

Results:____

____

____

____

____

My personal evaluation:___________________________

____

____

____

____

____

____

____

____

____

____

____

____

____

____

____

Date:_________________   Time:_________________

Environmental conditions and temperature:___________

____

____

____

____

Ingredients:_____________________________________

____

____

____

____

____

____

____

Special procedures, or other considerations:___________

____

____

____

____

Bottle type used:_________________________________

____

____

Headspace allowed:_______________________________

KT type and description:____________________________

____

____

Duration of secondary:_______________________________

____

____

Other information:___________________________________

____

____

____

____

Results:____

____

____

____

My personal evaluation:_______________________________

____

____

____

____

____

____

____

____

____

____

____

____

____

Date:_________________   Time:_________________

Environmental conditions and temperature:___________

____

____

____

____

Ingredients:______________________________________

____

____

____

____

____

____

____

Special procedures, or other considerations:___________

____

____

____

____

Bottle type used:_________________________________

____

____

Headspace allowed:_______________________________

KT type and description:___________________________

____

____

Duration of secondary:____________________________

____

____

Other information:______________________________

____

____

____

____

Results:_____________________________________

____

____

____

My personal evaluation:_________________________

____

____

____

____

____

____

____

____

____

____

____

____

CHAPTER 10: I'VE GOT MY OWN RECIPES NOW!

This is where you make this book really your own. In this area, you can record the successful results of your experiments from Chapter 9 that you would like to repeat in the future. Recording them here will make them readily available to you, and will give you the satisfaction of being able to produce sodas that are uniquely yours whenever you want, and for any occasion you want.

Just like in Chapter 9, you can write in the following pages, and you can download more pages in a variety of formats from the website: http://ToolsfortheJourney.com/2nd-brew-bonus. If you already downloaded the Experiment Records for Chapter 9, you do not need to do it again. The file contains both sets of documents. Likewise, if you are reading this as an eBook, you will see one page to show you the format, and can download the documents to create your own recipe book.

Please share your favorite recipe creations! You may post them at http://ToolsfortheJourney.com/recipes.   If we get enough really good ones, I will produce a crowd-sourced recipe book.

Since you are probably very familiar with typical recipe formats, I will only explain the elements that are unique to Kombucha.

"Type and Description of Kombucha Tea used:"
This provides information about the KT from the primary

fermentation. The "Type" should include the type of tea and sugar that were used. The "Description" should explain the sugar and acetic acid ("vinegar") content of the KT. This can be subjective ("semi-sweet", "very strong vinegar", etc.), or it can be objective observations, such as the pH. It might also include any information that would help you, or others, successfully reproduce the soda. For example, you might have found this recipe works best if the KT has been brewed for a longer time at a low temperature.

"Notes and comments:"

Add anything else that might help ensure the success and enjoyment of this recipe.

Date:_______________________

Recipe name:____

Description:____

____

____

____

Number of servings:________   Serving size:______________
Preparation time:________ Total time to serving:__________
Type and Description of Kombucha Tea used:__________

____

____

Ingredients:____

____

____

____

____

____

Instructions:____

____

____

____

____

____

Notes and comments:____

____

____

____

____

Date:___________________

Recipe name:____

Description:____

____

____

____

Number of servings:________ Serving size:____________
Preparation time:________ Total time to serving:________
Type and Description of Kombucha Tea used:________

____

____

Ingredients:____

____

____

____

____

____

Instructions:_______________________________________

____

____

____

____

____

Notes and comments:________________________________

____

____

____

____

Date:_________________

Recipe name:____

Description:____

____

____

____

Number of servings:_______   Serving size:____________
Preparation time:_______ Total time to serving:_________
Type and Description of Kombucha Tea used:__________

____

____

Ingredients:____

____

____

____

____

____

Instructions:____

____

____

____

____

____

Notes and comments:_________________________________

____

____

____

____

Date:_______________

Recipe name:_________________________________

Description:_________________________________

____

____

____

Number of servings:_______ Serving size:___________
Preparation time:_______ Total time to serving:_______
Type and Description of Kombucha Tea used:________

____

____

Ingredients:_________________________________

____

____

____

____

____

Instructions:_________________________________

____

____

____

____

____

Notes and comments:_________________________________

____

____

____

____

Date:_____________________

Recipe name:____

Description:____

____

____

____

Number of servings:________   Serving size:_____________
Preparation time:_________   Total time to serving:__________
Type and Description of Kombucha Tea used:___________

____

____

Ingredients:____

____

____

____

____

____

Instructions:____

____

____

____

____

____

Notes and comments:_________________________________

____

____

____

____

Date:_______________

Recipe name:____

Description:____

____

____

____

Number of servings:________   Serving size:_____________
Preparation time:________ Total time to serving:_________
Type and Description of Kombucha Tea used:_________

____

____

Ingredients:____

____

____

____

____

____

Instructions:____

____

____

____

____

____

Notes and comments:__________________________________

____

____

____

____

RESOURCES

I do not have any affiliation with any of these resources, and I cannot verify their veracity. Please do your own research. Some of these links may have become broken links by the time you read this. However, they do show how you can find resources with a little searching. Kombucha is becoming very popular and with some creativity, you should be able to locate what you need. If you do find a good reliable resource for anything related to KT, please let me know so I can include it in my next update.

You may write me at:
Guide1@ToolsForTheJourney.com

Kitchen Science" Experiment Record" and the *"My Recipes"* entry form: http://ToolsfortheJourney.com/2nd-brew-bonus

The Happy Herbalist
https://www.happyherbalist.com/kombucha/starter-kits/

http://free-kombucha.weebly.com/free-kombucha-exchange.html

http://www.kombuchafuel.com/2010/07/kombucha-scoby-exchange-on-facebook_14.html

https://kombuchaexchange.blog/

http://kombucha.ning.com/

ABOUT THE AUTHOR

Dale Gillilan has been on a quest since he was a young child, when he had a clear vision and understanding of his life's purpose and mission. He is a sociologist by training, and has always been driven by two questions. One is to understand what makes people "tick" — why do they do the things they do? This question led him as a teenager into a deep study of psychology, and then sociology.

He has traveled to many countries, studied cultures and traditions, eventually training as a shaman in a very ancient tradition, and then spending five years in the deserts of the Southwest US being guided by a reclusive Native American medicine man. A Hawaiian Kahuna gave him the title of "po'i 'uhane", which means "soul catcher", because of the powerful and extensive work he has done in "soul retrieval".

He became a practicing clinical hypnotherapist, a master of energy healing systems, and the head of a martial art — all in his search to understand his fellow human, and to fulfill his purpose. His diverse training has given him a unique and unusual ability to identify and reveal the Divine within each person. This is not a just a "spark of the Divine." It is much greater and more powerful. As he often says, "If we understood who we really are, our lives would be much different." Part of his work is to help others understand their true identity and power.

His second question that drives his life is to understand his relationship with God, with the Divine, and to help others find the Divine within their own selves. This desire has led him to be a missionary and to be compassionate servant, both as a volunteer in many settings, and as a leader of non-profit organizations. He is an active Emeritus member of the governing council of a large international organization for youth that is celebrating it's 100th anniversary.

Dale's unique experience in diverse spiritual realms and traditions has given him rare insights into human nature and the commonality of spiritual experiences. He has shared his knowledge and understanding through workshops for government, corporate and religious leaders, as well as public trainings, and individual counseling. He is currently providing very intensive training to select individuals who are ready to acknowledge their true power and become quiet leaders in shifting the world and society.

He lives with his wife and youngest child, dividing their time between Alaska and Hungary.

9 786150 002385